Get A life

A how to book for developing and maintaining a purposeful life

DR. DAVID GREENLAW

FIRST EDITION

ISBN 9780982785850

Library of Congress Control Number: 2010933486

Published by
NewBookPublishing.com, a division of Reliance Media, Inc.
2395 Apopka Blvd., #200, Apopka, FL 32703
NewBookPublishing.com

Printed in the United States of America

INTRODUCTION

The simple act of believing in oneself can enable individuals to accomplish dreams that may, at first glance, seem impossible. The opposite is just as true; lack of self-belief has kept many from accomplishing. Many lives have been minimized because of the way people viewed themselves. I wrote this book for the express purpose of helping such individuals achieve the greatest possible self-actualization.

These nine chapters are designed to give you the reader, tools for a successful life journey. These tools, utilized carefully and applied consistently, will guide you to fulfill your potential. Diagrams for visual learners are included to strengthen the impact of every learning opportunity. Utilize all of these resources, because this is about you.

Actually, each of the nine chapters is a book by itself, but this is meant to be a guide book. Utilize it as such and each day put into practice what you learn, letting no circumstances or individuals minimize your life journey.

TABLE OF CONTENTS

CHAPTER 1

INTENTIONALITY

"Some people succeed because they desired to, but most people succeed because they are determined."

Elmer Towns

"**O**nce upon a time." Isn't that how all of your childhood stories began? The problem is, we grow up and realize the early stories of life, which may have ended well for the good guy, don't always happen that way for us. In fact, some of the most frequent questions people ask themselves are, "Why am I not more successful? Why don't I have more money, more of the good things of life? Why do others seem to succeed but I don't?" The real problem is that these are the wrong questions. The right questions are, "What does being a successful person mean to me, and how do I go about becoming one?"

There is an ancient story that will help us in our search for understanding. It goes back to a time when the nation of Israel was taken into captivity by the Babylonians. Of course we live in today's world, but the basic needs of people haven't changed a great deal over the centuries. So let's go back in time for a brief moment. Once the Israelites were in captivity, their greatest desire was to be free and return to their city, Jerusalem, which represented to them the core of their existence. Without it, they weren't even a people. During the seventy years they were in captivity, they never forgot Jerusalem. How they longed for this city, to see it and once more and to establish themselves there.

The day finally came when they were allowed to return to their city. There were, however, some problems. Those who were returning were not the same ones who had left. In fact, those returning had only heard stories about the city from relatives and friends who had died. But the day they left Babylon for Jerusalem was a glorious day. Excitement filled the air. Going home was on everyone's lips. As they crossed the hundreds of miles, excitement and expectation mounted in everyone. Even the children caught the spirit and added to it until, finally, one evening they crossed the last hill and saw Jerusalem.

What they saw was devastation. That old city was nothing but rubble. The walls were knocked down, the gates were burned, and the houses were piles of rubble. Their high expectations turned to dismay and discouragement, and they basically gave up. They had some help in compounding their discouragement from neighbors who told them the city could never be rebuilt. The Israelites believed their neighbors and started asking questions. You know the ones. "Why did I ever come here? What's going to happen to me now? Why did God do this to me?" These questions and many others were asked by family after family, person after person. And just as one person's excitement had kindled another's when they began their journey, discouragement now infected them like a plague and they gave up.

Such is the influence we have on one another. Hearing negative things over and over again causes us to begin thinking negatively. It's like the power a group of people has in suggesting to an individual that he doesn't look well. The person starts out feeling fine. However, when enough people suggest to him that he doesn't look well, his mind begins to convince his body that he isn't well. We have all heard stories of perfectly well people who have gone home feeling sick simply because enough people told them they didn't look well. The power of suggestion from one person to another is phenomenal but the power of self-suggestion is even greater. I like to call it "explosive," but more about that in a moment. First, we've got to return to Jerusalem and the Israelites.

When they arrived and saw the devastation, depression —the "oh, poor me" syndrome— immediately set in. They settled into a lifestyle that had all the trappings of a broken and beaten person, and went about their lives without purpose or direction. They grew detached, were involved but not actively participating. Passive, angry, and hurt, they felt a deep sense of despair, and life didn't seem worth living. But someone and something changed all that.

His name was Nehemiah, and he was the king's cupbearer. The importance of his job can't be overstated. He tasted all of the king's drinks before the king partook, as a protection. If someone put poison in the king's drink, the cupbearer would die because he tasted it first, but the king would be saved. More important, however, the cupbearer had daily access to the king, often becoming a counselor or confidant of the king.

Nehemiah also considered Jerusalem to be his home city. When word came back to him that nothing was being done to rebuild the ancient city, he wept. He shared his concern with the king and was given permission to go and rebuild it. He took guards, money, and authority with him. When he reached Jerusalem, he saw a pathetic sight. Not only was the city in ruins, but the lives of the people who had originally returned to it were also in ruins.

If I told you that under Nehemiah's leadership the walls and the gates of that city were completed in just fifty-two days, would you believe me? Well, it's true. He accomplished in less than two months what others believed could never be done. What made the difference? Intentionality. (This may be a new word for you, but let me explain what the word means and how it works.)

The word "intentionality" implies that one has intentions, purposes, and goals or definite plans for his or her life. For most of us, the dawning of a need for goals and purpose may never happen or may come at a later stage of life. We have grown up in a society that encourages individualism up to a point, but tends to stifle creative thinking. All children start school at roughly the same age, learn the same subjects, and leave school at the same time. They learn a lot about different subjects but very little about themselves. And they learn nothing concerning their own value and capabilities or how they can make a meaningful contribution to life for themselves and others. But it's not too late to start.

My family and I spent a number of years living in sub-Saharan Africa. I taught at a college and learned many new and beautiful things about my students. I want to tell you one man's story, because he understood intentionality.

He was born in the small country of Malawi and grew up in the bush. He tended his father's cattle and went to primary school. At a very early age he knew that obtaining an education was essential for him, so he studied hard and finished twelve grades. He wanted to go to college, but there wasn't one anywhere near him, so he walked six hundred miles through strange and dangerous country to get to a college. Without money or much of anything else, he worked his way through school and graduated. Wanting to do more for his people, he came to America where he finished a master's and doctor's degrees. Today, he influences the education of thousands of young people all over East Africa. He had purpose and motivation. He had intentionality. How can you develop it? Hang on. We'll work on that now.

When the people first left for Jerusalem, they had a goal, which was to return home. However, when they arrived, they didn't find what they expected. Because of that, discouragement set in and they gave up. Keep in mind that they had all the tools for success with them. Some of them were stone masons, some were carpenters, so they could have rebuilt the city. The potential for success was there, so why didn't it happen? Because they didn't believe that they could do it. If you don't believe that you can do something, then you won't be able to do it. They lost their sense of personal mission, refused to set any goals, and failed in their minds before they ever began.

We suffer from the same problem. We let our minds convince us that we can't do something. Once that happens, we never will do it. For many, goal setting is a "dirty word," for it requires us to do things others say we can't do. Many would rather fail without beginning than fail while trying. But you can change all that. You can set goals and you can succeed. Here's how. First, set small goals that you know you can achieve. Next, tell yourself you can do it, act upon it and do it. After it's done, make sure you reward yourself for doing a good job.

Let me give you an example. The first time you sit down at the piano, you're not going to be able to play classical music. In fact, there won't be any class to your music at all. If, however, you take lessons, learn the keyboard, and learn where the notes are, you will gradually play music. In other words, set realistic goals and accomplish them one by one. Then you can ultimately accomplish big goals. You can learn to believe in yourself. That's what "intentionality" means: believing in yourself, acting upon that belief, setting realistic goals, and making them happen.

The other part of intentionality is having a sense of personal mission. Let's go back to Nehemiah and see why he was able to motivate the people when they felt it couldn't be done. He believed with all his being that the city was meant to be rebuilt. He believed that nothing could keep it from happening except people who didn't believe in the same mission. When Nehemiah first arrived at Jerusalem, he refused to see Jerusalem as destroyed, but chose instead to see it in its first phase of rebuilding. Then he began inspiring the people, telling them it was possible, and working beside them to make it possible. Through his power of suggestion and constantly telling the people they could do it, his goal became a reality. The power of one person suggesting to another that he can succeed empowers and gives permission for success to become a reality.

Now, I want to return to something I said earlier: The power of suggestion from one person to another is phenomenal, but the power of suggestion from yourself to yourself is greater, even explosive. By that, I mean you can learn to make yourself do the impossible. There are many stories about individuals who have overcome tremendous odds to succeed.

I know a man who lost his forearm and hand in an accident when he was about ten years old. His father operated a sawmill and had a shingle cutting tool that was like an automatic knife. The wood was put in to be shaped, then the knife cut it, and the wood was removed. Workers developed a certain rhythm. But the boy got out of rhythm with the machine, and it took off his arm and hand. When I met him, he was in his seventies and I really came to admire him. He had a hook where the hand should have been and could use it in amazing ways. Watching him, I was almost jealous that I didn't have a hook! He drove big trucks, loaded hay, logged, and did amazing things. My point is, he didn't let his loss cripple his mind, so it wasn't able to stop his body.

You cannot simply just let life "happen" to you. You must take control of it. You must decide that there is a worthy cause in life and realize that the greatest, most worthy cause is developing yourself—because, if you don't believe in you, nobody else will.

When I talk about being motivated to succeed, I want you to understand that I am not saying success is the same thing as money. For me, success means living a meaningful and purposeful life and being able to accomplish the tasks I set out to do. Success is also helping others to live meaningfully and purposefully. You see, the building of our lives is like the rebuilding of Jerusalem— sometimes painful and difficult but, in the end, beautiful more than worth the effort.

"When we are motivated by goals that have deep meaning, by dreams that need completion, by pure love that needs expressing, then we truly live life."

— Greg Anderson, US basketball player

What can I do?

Maintain a positive attitude

Use positive affirmations

Focus on doable goals

Concentrate on my successes

Things to do to motivate my-self:

1.

2.

3.

INTENTIONALITY PROCESS

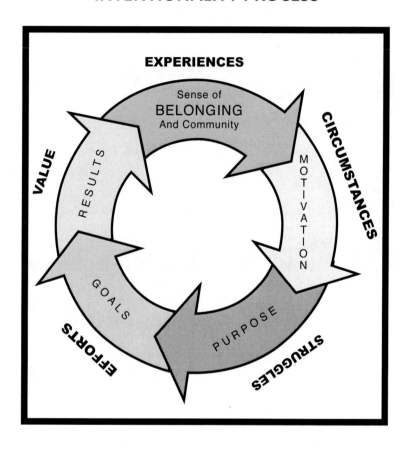

"I am not afraid of storms for I am learning
how to sail my ship."

Louisa May Alcott

CHAPTER 2

WELCOME TO OUR WORLD: NOT VERY NICE

"A self trust is a trust in God himself."

Ralph Waldo Emerson

Have you ever wondered if you really belong in this world? So often the demands we face and the signals we get from our society tell us there must be something wrong with us. Think for a moment about what our society says makes us valuable: driving the right car, living in the right neighborhood, being youthful, having lots of money, or, in other words, having all the "right" stuff. Too often, when we look at what we have and who we are, we just don't seem to measure up. We don't seem to have enough money and maybe we don't have the best education and we all get old. Over and over, the information we get keeps telling us that we don't have what it takes.

In our society, the problem of low self-esteem has reached epic proportions. Some researchers claim that upwards of ninety percent of our population suffer from it. People simply don't believe in themselves, which makes it very hard for them to believe in anyone else. So we wear masks and play "let's pretend" games. Because of this we struggle with life and never feel successful.

Let me introduce you to Jackie. She is twenty-seven years old, has two children, and is divorced. She is very attractive and capable of accomplishing many things well. The problem is that she doesn't think so. She sees herself as a first class failure; if something she does turns out very well, she won't take credit for it. Jackie does not believe in Jackie. She is divorced and thinks that is her fault, as well. Why? Why does she approach life this way?

When Jackie was growing up, the significant people in her life told her that she couldn't do anything right. She could never please her demanding mother, who constantly told her she was homely and undesirable. When things went wrong at home, she was told that she was responsible, that it was somehow her fault. By hearing this over and over from her family, she began to believe it. Worse, she began to act her beliefs out in her life. She felt that she deserved to be put down and that she was the cause of most problems. When her divorce took place she believed it was her fault. Even though she was being physically, sexually and emotionally abused, Jackie felt that she was getting what she deserved.

Jackie came to my office because she was getting married again and didn't want a repeat of the past. After we talked for some time, I asked her to go to a large mirror on my wall and look herself directly in the eyes. But she simply couldn't do it. She obediently looked into the mirror but not with eye-to-eye contact. I then asked her to tell herself that she was a valuable person.

After standing for the longest time at the mirror, she

finally began to weep. "I can't say that, because it isn't true," she finally cried out. Having been told often enough by the significant people in her life that she wasn't valuable, she believed them and acted upon it. Now, after months of counseling, she can look herself in the eyes and tell herself she's valuable, but it will be a long time before she is totally healed… if she ever is.

The problem, of course, is that we are using the wrong standard to measure what makes us valuable. If this standard is youth, education, money and the like, then we are all in trouble. We must base our self-worth on something better. The basis of good self-esteem is really very simple and can best be stated in this way: I exist as a human being, therefore, I have absolute worth. It is only when we catch this truth that our own value and the value of others comes into focus. As children, many of us were taught, "God didn't make no junk."

Positive self-esteem then means that no matter what I do, no matter my race, height or age, I am a valuable person because my value isn't based on things, but on the intrinsic value of being. With this assurance, I am free to be myself and contribute my unique qualities to life.

I am not saying that the building or rebuilding of your life will be all fun and games. I will say, however, that it is worth the effort, because you are worth the effort. Although you may continue to get lots of negative feedback from society and friends, you must develop a new way of dealing with yourself. I am going to give you seven steps that will help you in this building process. I have chosen seven because there are seven days in the week. And by using the weekly cycle, you can learn to practice these every day of the week.

Seven Steps to healing and developing a good self-image

Step One: Practice thinking about yourself in positive ways. The way we think about ourselves comes out in the way we talk about ourselves and the way we treat ourselves. We say things like, "I don't deserve this," "That's too good for me," or "I could never accomplish anything meaningful."

Stop for a moment and consider all the negative information you feed yourself about yourself every day. Take a piece of paper and list all the things you do well and that give you a feeling of accomplishment. Don't be modest. Maybe you are a good carpenter, housekeeper, mechanic, or dishwasher. Tell yourself that you do these things well. Learn to focus on the positive aspects of who you are and what you do, as opposed to the negative.

Our minds are wonderful computers. They store the information we feed in and constantly return it to us when we want or need it. The problem is that the storage system doesn't know positive information from negative information. Therefore, if you tell yourself only negative things about yourself and associate only with people who give you negative feedback, you will constantly hear nothing but negativism. To counter this, you should start playing positive messages.

How aware are you of the routine you go through every morning when you get up. Take tying your shoes, for example. You do it so often, that you don't even think about it. Unfortunately, thinking negative thoughts about yourself happens the same way. If you think negatively long enough, the process becomes automatic. Fortunately, however, the opposite is also true. Positive thinking and positive feedback from significant people forces our minds to send us positive information.

There are numerous stories of people whose lives have been changed by positive thinking. These stories all find their source in the fact that the individuals chose to think positively about themselves and acted upon that belief.

For example, I know a man who wanted to be a race car driver. Stock car racing had been his big dream since he was a child. He helped rebuild cars, went to the track, and did everything he could to be a race car driver. The problem was that nobody would let him drive a race car, because he had a birth defect: one of his arms was useless and it simply hung by his side. The other arm was powerful and capable, but he was told driving with one arm was impossible. In the minds of most people, it was impossible, but he always saw himself as a driver and a winner. Eventually you guessed it, he found a way. He even became the state champion. In other words, he did what he'd been told was impossible. You can do it, too!

Step two is deciding for yourself what success is, and not allowing others to impose their standards of success on you. We seem to be able to define success only in terms of money and possessions. The conclusions we reach, therefore, inform us that if we have a lot of money and things, then we are successful, and if we don't, then we are not.

But what is success? Success is being and doing what I want to do and doing it to the best of my ability. It may be raising your children to become responsible adults. It may be becoming the best plumber or carpenter or salesman that you can be. There have been many great teachers, churchmen, and local community leaders who made tremendous contributions to life but didn't have a large number of earthly possessions.

There is a simple diagram that has helped me to keep on track for my own standard of success. It is one of those tools that is passed down from person to person and for which no one can truly take credit. So I use it here, hoping that the exercise will be helpful as you decide what success means to you. It looks like this:

The diagram below asks:

Question 1. Who am I?

Question 2. Who do I want to be?

Question 3. What keeps me from being who I want to be?

Question 4. How do I get rid of what keeps me from
being who I want to be?

Who am I?	Who do I want to be?
1	2
3	4
What blocks me?	How do I remove the blocks?

In window one, answer the question in words or symbols, then move on to windows two, three, and four. If you are honest with yourself, you will find this tool helpful in formulating answers to your questions about what success and life means to you.

Step three is learning to set goals that are realistic and can be accomplished. When you are dealing with yourself you need to be honest. For example, if at age fifty-five you decide you want to be a brain surgeon but you haven't been to college yet, you probably aren't being realistic and honest with yourself. In other words, you are setting yourself up to fail. Of course, if you have no goals at all, you have also set yourself up to fail. The reality is that we need to set realistic goals, some that we can easily achieve and some that make us stretch and struggle. We also need short-term and long-term goals. Accomplishing goals helps us feel like a success, but the goals we set must be realistic.

A man I know wanted to be in upper-level management in a certain international company. However, he didn't have the experience or education to qualify him for that position. When an entry-level position in the company became available, he accepted it. One of his goals was achieved; he was working for the company. Whenever an opportunity to develop himself and better understand the company business came along, he enthusiastically went for it. In his late forties, he retired from the company as one of its top executives and started his own business. By setting and working on short-term goals, he ultimately reached his long-term goal.

As a college professor, I saw many older students finally graduate. When asked how they did it, their reply was always the same, "One subject at a time." Success in each small or short-term goal ultimately allowed them to succeed in accomplishing their larger or long-term goals.

Step four is positive self-talk. Learning to self-praise, both to ourselves and others, seems to be difficult for most of us. We don't want to seem boastful or arrogant, so we tend not to talk about our positive actions and attributes. In our society, there is a great deal of concentration on the negative. In fact, children are often told they are stupid, incapable, and unlovable. With all the negative information we receive, no wonder we are hard-pressed to speak positively to ourselves. It's time to tell yourself you are a valuable person. If you do it often enough, you will not only start believing it, but you will also start acting upon that belief. This is because what we say about ourselves to ourselves and to others eventually becomes easy for us to believe and to act upon.

Take credit for your accomplishments and successes, and remember that failures may not be your fault. Believe in yourself and apply yourself to your tasks. And don't forget to congratulate yourself on your competency.

Step five is to focus on what you do well and to accept the praise that goes with a job well done. If I asked you to make a list of things that you do not do very well, you could probably do that very quickly. If, however, I asked you to list five things you do well, you would probably have difficulty listing that many. Of course, none of us will ever be able to do everything, let alone do everything well. That puts us all in the same situation. But just because we can't do everything well doesn't mean we aren't valuable. It does, however, mean that we need to focus on what we can do well. So quit comparing yourself with the superstars. Instead learn to be in competition with yourself and stop worrying about competing with everyone else.

Step six is to be involved constantly in self-improvement. Self-improvement comes from many different sources, obtaining a formal education, learning new hobbies, and gaining a better understanding of people, among others. But we must all be involved in a lifelong pursuit to improve ourselves.

When I was in my early teens I hated woodworking. Maybe it was because my dad enjoyed it and because I hated to sand. But whatever the reason, I convinced myself I didn't like it. Part of the problem was the discipline it takes to keep at the details of a woodworking project until it is not just finished, but done well. Over the years, however, I have developed a love for making furniture. Now, it gives me a great deal of pleasure to see tables, beds, and other articles as finished products. It hasn't always been easy to follow through and make myself do better work, but it is imperative that I do so, because self-improvement raises my self-esteem.

Step seven involves focusing on other people. This step can best be described as seeing others in a positive way and doing everything we can to build them up. The effects of doing this are almost magical. Treating others positively starts a chain reaction that ultimately comes back to us, and we are treated positively in return. Even more importantly, by so relating we set others on a journey that allows them to experience the joys of a meaningful existence. We tend to believe that what we feel and the insecurities we experience are unique to us, but that isn't so. We live in a society that puts us down- one in which we often don't measure up and fall short of our own expectations. But we must not let the life around us control us. We must take control and make life happen to us. These seven steps are but introductions to a more meaningful life a life that is valuable, productive, focused- a life that is me.

"Remember that you are the stars and the stars are you."
Poems by Joy Harjo. Know yourself, understand yourself, heal your personality and develop self awareness. A more meaningful life awaits you.

What can I do?

Pampering

Get control over your imagination

Utilize self-evaluation

Be assertive

Map out your personal journey to self-improvement

HEALING TOWARDS A POSITIVE SELF-ESTEEM

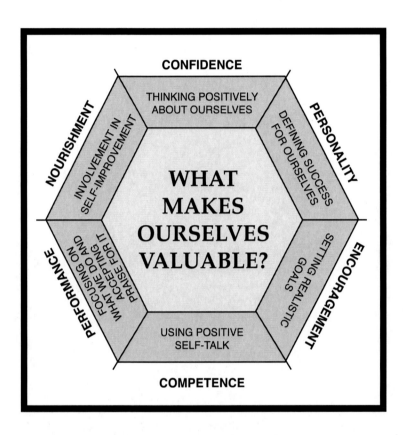

"When you do the common things in life in an uncommon way, you will command the attention of the world."

George Washington Carver

CHAPTER 3

UNDERSTANDING OURSELVES AND OTHERS

"A great man shows his greatness by the way he treats little men."

Thomas Carlyle

Every person born into this world is a unique individual. There has never been anyone who is exactly like you or me, and there never will be. All of us have something special to share that society has never before been privileged to have, and that something special is us.

There are some similarities among and differences between people that help us understand why we react and interact with others the way we do. The effort to try to define human temperament and behavior has been going on for centuries. The Greeks used the terms: Melancholy, Choleric, Phlegmatic, and Sanguine to define various behavior patterns. In recent years, there has been a steady increase in the understanding and use of temperaments as a means to help people understand themselves and others. Prominent psychologists have developed inventories that help people understand their temperament and discover the implications of these inventories on how they approach life.

I want to use these old Greek terms and describe

behavior that corresponds to them so you can understand yourself better. We will explore the leadership style that fits each temperament and see how each one interacts with the others. First, however, let me say that humans are much more complex than a simple category. For instance we know that elements of the four basic temperament categories inhabit all of us to a greater or lesser degree. And we know we have one temperament that dominates and another that backs it up. But before we go too far, let me give you some background and definitions that will be helpful.

As you can see from the diagram at the end of the chapter, our first step is to divide people into two main groups, the extroverts and the introverts. Extroverts are interested in what is going on in the world around them, have an interest in people other than themselves, are usually active and expressive, and want to be involved in what is going on around them. An introvert, on the other hand, tends to direct their attention on themselves. They tend to be less involved in the world around them, and concern themselves instead with how their environment affects them.

We have all experienced these differences in ourselves and others. Next time you are at a party, notice those who easily mix with others and those who are more reticent in presenting themselves. Extroverts tend to know and socialize with a lot of people, but do not usually allow their relationships to become very deep. Introverts, on the other hand, have a smaller circle of friends but want those relationships to have depth and commitment.

Now, let's explore the four terms we borrowed from the Greeks and see if we can make them come alive. I will give you descriptions of the positive and negative characteristics of each temperament and then put faces with them.

I want to begin with the **Sanguine**, because that type is very easy to spot. They are people lovers and enjoy the attention that the limelight brings to them. They can be found wherever there is a crowd, and they usually talk more than they listen. It is very important to extroverts that people like them. To satisfy this need, they usually become what is known as a "people pleaser." Words that help us understand and define extroverts would be:

POSITIVE		NEGATIVE
Cheerful	Dynamic	Unorganized
Sincere	Friendly	Superficial
Optimistic	Carefree	Restless
Compassionate	Enthusiastic	Pleaser
Sociable	Spontaneous	Glad-hander

Sanguines are also very feeling persons and, as you can see in the diagram, they show emotions very readily. Because people are important to them, it is necessary that they work in a people environment. To place them in an office and ask them to do only detail work is to set them up to fail. They must interact with others. Sanguines make good salespeople, public speakers, promoters, and leaders. Their attention span is often short, so they need to learn to focus and concentrate in order to accomplish the task at hand.

An individual who represented many of the Sanguine qualities well was Will Rogers, the great American humorist and social critic. There is no doubt that he was a lover of people, an excellent actor, and a real "stage" person. He wrote books and a newspaper column, and spent most of his time entertaining people. His life focus was being around and interacting with people. The statement for which he is best know, "I never met a man I didn't like," is the essence of being Sanguine.

The second temperament is the other extrovert, the **Choleric**. Although extroverted, Cholerics have a totally different approach to life. These are take charge individuals who intend to be in control. Words that help us understand and define them would be:

POSITIVE		NEGATIVE
Productive	Energetic	Angry
Pragmatic	Strong-willed	Domineering
Decisive	Adventure lovers	Aggressive
Tenacious	Confident	Proud
Organized		Self-sufficient
Perceptive		Insensitive

Probably the greatest single capability of the Choleric's leadership is also that temperament's weakness. They know where they are going and they know how to get there. The problem is they may leave a string of hurt people behind them. Their insensitivity to the feelings of others, coupled with their anger, often keeps them from accomplishing their goals. A classic example of a Choleric is General George S. Patton. He was one of the most colorful generals of World War II. He easily took charge, and expected people to follow his direction. He also was outspoken and reckless, and there was never any question as to who was in command. Known by his men as "Old Blood and Guts," he is remembered by many in the Western world for the two soldiers suffering from battle neurosis that he slapped while visiting an Army hospital in 1943.

If you give Cholerics a task to do, then make sure you give them the authority to carry it out. They make good leaders, but must constantly be reminded that people are more important than anything else in life. It is also necessary that they learn to appreciate other temperament types and allow them the freedom to be themselves.

We now focus on the two introverted temperaments which are as different from each other as the extroverts are. First, let's look at the **Phlegmatic**, a gentle-spirited individual who can best be described with words like these:

POSITIVE		NEGATIVE
Practical	Peaceable	Lazy
Tactful	Dry wit	Unprogressive
Dependable	Efficient	Slow
Flexible	Attentive	Indecisive
Calm	Diplomatic	Stubborn

The Phlegmatic goes through life without getting ulcers, but often gives them to others. To the extroverts, the Phlegmatic doesn't move quickly enough or accomplish enough, but he or she does counterbalance a lot of the extrovert negatives. Phlegmatics are good listeners and make good counselors, because they don't jump to conclusions or stick their noses in other people's business.

To best describe this individual, I will use the example of a dear friend whom I greatly value. For purposes of discussion (and to retain the friendship), let's call him "Bill." He is a very accomplished businessman with all of the positive characteristics of the Phlegmatic, but he drives me crazy when it comes to making decisions. For the last two years, he has been shopping for a new car. He has read all the reports on many makes and models, has test-driven a wide variety of cars, but still hasn't decided which one to buy. At this rate he will never buy a new car, because anything he might be seriously considering will be obsolete before he makes up his mind!

Our last basic temperament is the **Melancholy**. Words that best describe this group are:

POSITIVE		NEGATIVE
Creative	Gifted	Moody
Idealistic	Sensitive	Critical
Loyal	Conscientious	Unsociable
Precise	Analytical	Rigid
Self-sacrificing	Theoretical	Pessimistic

Without the Melancholies, life would lack the aesthetic and the beautiful. They are truly creative, well-focused and good thinkers, but they are never satisfied. They want to live in a perfect world and so demand perfection from themselves. But, because our world is imperfect, they often feel discouraged or depressed.

Leonardo daVinci portrayed this temperament well. He was born in Florence, Italy, during the early stages of the Renaissance and was truly a Renaissance man. He was an inventor, engineer, artist, sculptor, and much more. During his lifetime, he was considered one of the best painters in Italy. His problem was that he was rarely satisfied with what he did, especially with his painting. Over and over, he would leave pictures unfinished, because he was not happy with the work he had done. He was a true perfectionist accomplishing little, because he didn't feel he could do anything well enough.

The Melancholy loves detail work and works very well alone at detail tasks without becoming bored. Melancholics need to be encouraged to use their creativity and helped to see that not everything can be perfect. This is especially true when they are dealing with people, with whom they too often lack patience, because people are not and cannot be perfect.

So those are the four basic temperaments. But, as I previously mentioned, no one is a perfect example of any one of the four. We contain characteristics of all four, but one type is usually dominant. This allows for sixteen different possibilities, and understanding   each one is fascinating. And even more fascinating are the ways in which they interact with one another.

With some people extroverted, others introverted, some

Choleric, others Melancholy, is it any wonder that we have problems relating to one another? The obvious key here is to understand that no one type is better than the others. We are who we are, and must learn to accept our strengths and work to diminish our weaknesses. As we accomplish this, we will be more accepting of those who approach life differently than we do.

I grew up in a family of seven boys (that's right, seven boys!) and no girls. We seven boys are all alike, and yet so different. We grew up in the same home, attended the same schools and, lived in the same town, but each of us is unique and different from each other. The four different temperaments can be seen in each of us. We have different vocations and married wives with different perspectives on life, yet we are all brothers who care deeply for, and about, each other. Thus it must be for all of us in life: We must recognize our differences but learn to develop and care for one another.

Have fun, be silly, and feel good about being you and being alive in this world!

What can I do?

Keep a Journal

What is your temperament style?

UNDERSTANDING OURSELVES
AND OTHERS

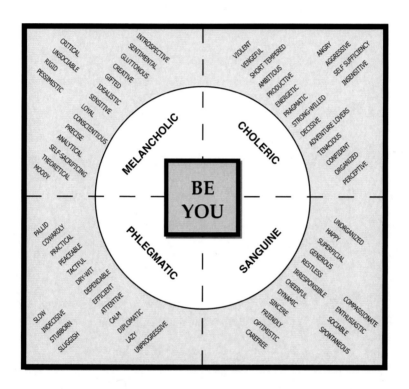

"The most effective way to achieve right relationships is to look for the best in every person, and then help that best into its fullest expression."

Allen J. Boone

CHAPTER 4

MANAGEMENT BY VALUE

*"Try not to be a person of success but rather,
a person of value."*

Albert Einstein

We are all leaders, whether we want to be or not. Some of us are called upon to lead in our chosen vocations; others are involved in community affairs. Most of us are leaders within our families, and certainly we are leaders of our selves. The problem is that many people are unsuccessful in their leadership endeavors because they don't understand how their management style affects the very people they want to lead. In this chapter, we will explore the ways in which our temperament is directly related to our style of leadership and the problems that can result. We will also discuss the things we can change to improve our interactions and bring about the results we want.

How much simpler life would be if all management styles were based on the Golden Rule, "Do unto others as you would have them do unto you." But because we often don't understand how our leadership affects and influences other people, we simply assume that we are operating by the Golden Rule meanwhile, the perception of those we are attempting to lead is just the opposite. They feel they are being treated as things rather than people; and being used to fulfill our needs and desires. What then are the values we must keep in mind as we deal with and lead individuals in our private, public or vocational lives? Here are the issues to keep in mind as we develop into leaders and managers.

One: People are more important than things. This means that we should not use people to achieve our goals, but we should learn to help others reach their goals. In the process, they will help us reach ours, because people who feel valued give much more than those who feel used.

Two: Human beings have two basic psychological needs: recognition and reward. When we fulfill these basic needs, people are only too happy to give. Remember what it feels like to be recognized for something you have done and how pleasant the reward was! Other people need that affirmation, as well.

So how do different temperaments lead and what are the results? Let's look at a diagram and then I will give you the answers in detail.

TEMPERAMENT AND MANAGEMENT STYLES

PEOPLE ARE MORE IMPORTANT THAN THINGS

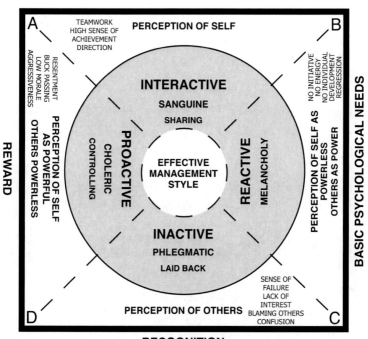

RECOGNITION

"The growth and development of people is the highest calling of leadership"

Harvey S. Firestone

This diagram has to do with power and our perception of ourselves and those around us. It also shows how those of different temperaments see themselves in relationship to power. The circle is divided into quarters, with line AD representing the way you view yourself and line BC representing those you live and work with. Quarter AB represents the person who sees himself as having power and people around him as powerless without him. This person usually assumes a management style that is best described as controlling, and has the temperament style that best fits the Choleric. He always wants to be in charge, and sees himself as having all the answers and others as needing to be told what to do.

Let me give you four words to describe the characteristics of this management style with its results:

CONTROLLING CHARACTERISTICS	RESULTS
Obedience	Resentment
Policy	Buck-passing
Tells	Low morale
Bossy ways	Aggressiveness

Thus we see that the Choleric, who likes to interact with people, is the one in control, but he really doesn't get what he wants. The response he engenders in others creates an unhealthy atmosphere.

The next piece of the circle is represented by quarter BD. This individual sees himself and others as having no power to accomplish anything or change his surroundings or his life.

Most of his energy is used simply to survive. He never really feels in charge and when he is, he doesn't take the opportunity to develop his leadership capabilities. The following are characteristics and results of this style:

LAID-BACK CHARACTERISTICS	RESULTS
No direction	Sense of failure
Lack of goals	Lack of interest
No sense of responsibility	Blaming others
Niceness	Confusion

The Phlegmatic individuals fall into this category more easily than anyone else. They make the mistake of believing that they are not going to accomplish a great deal by their actions or leadership, so they simply let others lead or let circumstances and situations drift. Believing that others can survive without direction, they create not only confusion but also a sense of no accomplishment, and nothing gets done.

The third piece of the circle is represented by quarter CD. This management style is best described as believing that everyone else has more power. It doesn't come from a lack of capability on the part of the leader, but from the leader's perception of self. Because these types tend to be perfectionistic, they feel that they never do anything well enough. They have high standards for themselves and for others, but the standards they set for themselves are always more demanding. Never feeling that they have accomplished their goals, they become reactive rather than pro-active to life. Instead of feeling in control, they feel controlled. This negative sense of self does amazing things to their management style. You would expect them to give up and not lead. Instead, they become passive- aggressive and show many of the characteristics of the Choleric. The reactive leadership style looks like this:

REACTIVE CHARACTERISTICS	RESULTS
Demands loyalty	No initiative
Seizes power	No energy
Wants control	No individual development
Acts parental	Regression

This leadership or management style best describes the Melancholy temperament. In their desire to do things correctly, Melancholics tend to forget that people are important, and not merely objects used to perform a task.

The last quarter in the circle is AC. I have called this the sharing management style. This style sees everyone as being in need of power. It allows all to share in that power and accomplish the tasks together. The shared leadership is best summarized like this:

SHARING CHARACTERISTICS	RESULTS
Power sharing	Teamwork
High sense of achievement	Accomplishment
Group goals	Direction
Brotherly/sisterly actions	Friendship

Because Sanguine, have a great need for people and want to be liked, they tend to use this type of management style the most often.

Having described and labeled leadership styles and temperaments, let me say that although we are inclined by temperament to utilize one style more often, we can learn to use them all. Yes, that's correct. We should learn to utilize all of the leadership styles, because they are all useful, depending upon the situation in which we find ourselves.

Realizing that we deal with a variety of situations and people, we must be able to figure out how we can empower the individuals with whom we interact. Let's use the family unit as an example. Every child who becomes a part of a family needs to be treated as an individual. Here's why: An extroverted child does not have the same attention span as an introverted child and may require more of your time to train. If you send the Sanguine child out to mow the lawn and there is a ball game going on next door, he may well run over and play ball before he mows the lawn. As a result, you may punish him more often as you try to teach him the necessity of concentrating on and finishing his assigned tasks. An introverted child, on the other hand, may need only a disapproving look to help him remember what you wanted him to accomplish. To punish them both the same way is to help the one and hinder the other. In reality, as human beings are one big family we should be concerned for each another. If as a result, we as adults can learn that the way we treat people either builds them up or tears them down, we will soon consider it a privilege to help others grow. People working at many jobs and in many occupations feel they are being used by their bosses. This management style is a kind of means to an end, but it doesn't benefit workers so they don't perform at their best.

Part of the problem we have in building others up is that of our own self-worth. As I said earlier, all of us suffer with varying degrees of low self-esteem. Because we are fighting for our own identity and value, we don't have much energy left to build up other people. However, by recognizing our own needs and seeing the way our leadership style affects others, we will be able to change that which has been destructive into something empowering and ennobling.

Management by values then means a number of things. First of all, it means that I value my life so much that I believe in me and treat myself in nondestructive ways. I stop the negative self-talk and quit doing those things which put me down in my own mind. I constantly push my own horizons because I can do so if I try. Life has meaning because I have meaning. I don't constantly have to prove my value to others. I am content in the reality that because I live, I am valuable. Based on my belief, I am free to move outside of the focus on myself and begin to see the same value in my fellow human beings.

The second great aspect of management by values is my recognition that I need to build up others in order to reach my full potential. The way I manage people must be in keeping with my realization of their worth. They are as valuable as I am. Therefore, I will do nothing to put them down, but will endeavor to build them up. If industry would learn this secret about dealing with people and helping others to reach their goals, we would see a renewal in work ethics and craftsmanship.

Once we have learned to manage our lives by values and to do the same for those we rub shoulders with every day, we can begin to help others grow and to deal with some of the other problems that being human brings to all of us.

"The most self-destructive thought that any person can have is thinking that he or she is not in total control of his or her life. That's when 'Why me?' becomes a theme song."

— **Roger Dawson**

From the list below, mark five values that are most important to you. Then, if you only could mark two from those five as the last and most important to you which would those be.

ACHIEVEMENT	FRIENDSHIP	PHYSICAL CHALLENGE
Advancement and promotion	Growth	Pleasure
Adventure	Having a family	Power and authority
Affection (love and caring)		Privacy
Arts	Helping other people	Public Service
Challenging problems	Helping Society	Purity
Change and variety	Honesty and Independence	Quality of what I take part in
Close relationships	Influencing others	Quality of relationships
Community	Inner harmony	Recognition (respect from others, status)
Competence	Integrity	Religion
Competition	Intellectual status	Reputation
Cooperation	Involvement	Responsibility and Accountability
Country	Job tranquility	Security
Creativity	Knowledge	Self-respect
Decisiveness	Leadership	Serenity
Democracy	Location	Sophistication
Ecological awareness	Loyalty	Stability
Economic security	Market position	Status
Effectiveness	Meaningful work	Supervising others
Efficiency	Merit	Time freedom
Ethical practice	Money	Truth
Excellence	Nature	Wealth

CHAPTER 5

HOW TO LIVE WITH NEGATIVE PEOPLE

"Self assurances reassure others."

Garry Wills

They are out there. Everywhere you go, and every place you turn you will find negative people who throw a wet blanket over your ideas, and give you a thousand reasons why you will never succeed. Using themselves as examples, they become living proof that ordinary people cannot achieve success. Unfortunately, it's easy to buy into their negative ways and their reasons why you or your idea will fail. But you must forget about them and learn to see the positive possibilities. There are many reasons why some people are negative. Some are negative by temperament alone. For example, the two introverts, Melancholy and Phlegmatic, tend towards negativity. The Melancholy are negative because they live in an imperfect world and believe that no matter how well something turns out, it could have always been better. The Phlegmatic don't put enough energy forth to make something happen, and so conclude that it can't possibly happen. Many people hold on to past failures and present problems that keep them from believing, and pass their skepticism along to those around them.

When I was growing up, I knew a number of adults who always seemed to be negative. I especially remember one of my high school teachers who was certain that my generation was going to bring about the destruction of the civilized world. He had only a limited belief in those students who were academically excellent and spent every free moment studying. I didn't fall into that group, but I also wasn't on his list of those who he felt would surely end up crowding our prisons and becoming burdens on society. Those young men, who had their own cars to drive, wore their shirt collars turned up, and only came to class to keep a seat warm, were the real targets of his wrath. He constantly berated them and assured them that they would amount to nothing in life.

One such student, who fit his description of a loser perfectly, ended up very successful in life. He built an automotive business that has given him a lifestyle few others are privileged to enjoy. Years later, I asked this negative teacher how he explained the success of this particular student, and his reply was interesting. He said that he still believed his basic philosophy of doom, but once in a while someone would rise beyond his expectations and succeed. I asked my old teacher how this could happen and he replied that "the student must have refused to believe all the negative things I said to him."

Herein lies one of the keys to dealing with negative people: Don't believe the negative things they tell you, and learn to counter their negativism with positive, self-assuring thoughts. This isn't to say we shouldn't examine ourselves and listen to what others say about us, for doing so can provide us with opportunities for growth. There is, however, a tremendous difference between constructive criticism which builds you up and negative criticism from people who never see or say anything positive about you.

An understanding of the martial arts can help us refocus what we hear so we don't react to situations, but learn to focus on and evaluate them. A growing number of people around the world are learning martial arts as a means of self-defense, but even more are learning it as a form of self-discipline. It is not merely a training of the body; it is also a training of the mind. Martial arts is a form of unarmed combat that began in the Orient and its history can be traced as far back as 460 B.C.

One of the basic aspects of martial arts training is learning to focus or concentrate on your immediate surroundings and needs. The ability to focus clearly on one object or to give complete attention to one thing while much is going on around you helps to put the occurrences of life into perspective. Negative people do not focus. Instead, they listen to all the information that is being fed to them by a multitude of individuals and situations, become confused by it all and then react. Always having to react causes us to feel out of control, making them defensive and negative. On the other hand, focusing on and seeing issues one by one, with clarity, helps us to resolve the issues in our lives.

I am sure that you have seen, either on television or in a live demonstration, martial arts experts break boards or bricks with their bare fingers or hands. There is a secret to martial arts, and it's not strength. As a student of karate approaches the object to be broken, he or she blocks out everything else and focuses only on the object to be broken. In the process of concentration, the student envisions his or her hand or foot passing through the object to a point beyond. In the student's mind he or she never stops at the edge of the object, for doing so will bring only failure. Your body will go only as far as your mind will allow. "Seeing" your hand or foot slice through the board allows your mind to enable your body to accomplish the task.

Negative people do not envision themselves as winners. In their minds, they firmly believe that they can't succeed and, therefore, they won't. The extended aspect of this mentality is that misery loves company, so they become like prophets of doom spreading their poison everywhere they go.

It is so easy for us to get caught up in this process and become negative. The old axiom, "By beholding, we become changed," certainly applies here. The criticism and negativism of so many different people can be crushing to a sensitive individual, but you must not believe in what negative people say, you must believe in you.

How is it that, in the face of negativity, mankind has been able to invent so many wonderful things? Take Orville and Wilbur Wright for instance. Many, many people kept saying to them, "It can't be done. It can't be done. It's foolish! How can two men who are really bicycle builders put together something that will go up in the air and fly?" They constantly had to overcome in their own minds the negative influence coming to them from individuals who were putting down their ideas, who were negative, and were saying it couldn't happen. But on December 17, 1903, the world's first flight in a power-driven-heavier-than-air machine took place at Kitty Hawk, North Carolina. The life story of Thomas A. Edison is also a study in how one can overcome great adversity. In his early life, a constant barrage of people put him down saying that he would never amount to anything. People in the community were convinced that he was crazy; that he had mental deficiencies. Even his father had serious doubts about what young Thomas would amount to. But his mother believed in him and gave him the courage to rise above all of the negative information that was constantly being fed to him by significant people in his life- that someone was his mother. No matter what others said or how they criticized, his mother constantly affirmed him. Thomas Edison patented more than 2500 inventions. He invented things like electric lights, the phonograph, megaphone, movies, and the list goes on and on.

So many times, we see young people who struggle to accomplish something because the significant people in their lives have berated instead of encouraged them and kept them from doing and being all that they could. Whereas, if someone had come along who believed them and encouraged them, these young people may have made a tremendous contribution to the world in which they lived. The limitations that we face in life take place in our mind first, and then find their way into our actions. So, if you put or let others put limitations on you emotionally or mentally, and you accept these limitation as truth, then you will act and react to them.

So what do we do when negative people surround us? How do we live with them? How do we function when it seems as if they have tremendous power over us? First of all, it's important that we believe in ourselves. Remember, if you don't believe in yourself, nobody else will, either. Second, find someone who will also believe in you; someone who believes that all people have something positive to offer to society and the world. Next, you must focus upon the things around you that are positive and put as little emphasis as possible on the things that are negative. As you begin to do this, a strange and interesting thing will happen. You will find that the people who have been so negative in your life no longer hold the same kind of influence over you. Further, they will begin to approach you in a different manner as they begin to perceive you in a different light. The end result will be that they will treat you in more positive ways.

Finally, you must keep in mind that you are not going to give others the power to determine who or what you are. Negative people will always abound, but they must not be allowed to control the way in which you see yourself.

"No matter what happens, stay positive. With every breath, the possibility of a new aspect of self arises."
— Wayne Muller

What can I do?

Decondition a negative thought pattern.

BELIEVE IN YOURSELF AND IN YOUR CAPABILITIES

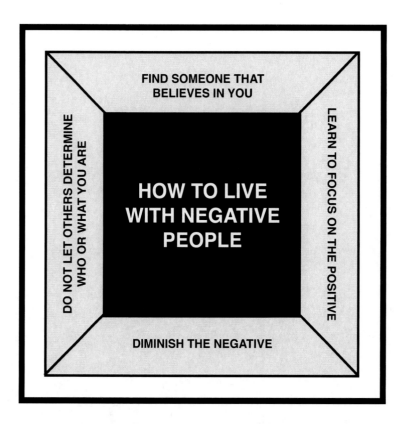

"The worst things in history have happened when people stop thinking for themselves, especially when they allow themselves to be influenced by negative people. That's what gives you dictators. Avoid that at all costs. Stop it first on a personal level, and you will have contributed to world sanity as well as your own."

Donald Trump

CHAPTER 6

QUIT BLAMING MOM AND DAD

"Blame is like lightning; it hits the highest."

Baltasar Gracia

There are so many ways of getting around accepting responsibility for my actions. If I can somehow convince myself that something is not my fault, then I can continue to act in whatever way I choose. In today's world, there is lots of support for the attitude, "I can't help it." We have all read books that seek to explain the brash behavior of an individual on the fact that his mother didn't change his diaper frequently enough. Let me list for you some of the excuses that are used most often, and see if you have ever heard any of them or maybe even used one or two.

    a) I was punished too hard when I was young.

    b) My parents never believed in me.

    c) We were poor and couldn't afford anything but the basics.

    d) I was the middle child.

    e) I was never given any opportunity.

    f) I am a member of a minority.

Many of us use these and other excuses every day to convince ourselves that our lack of success is really someone else's problem. I want to dispel that myth for you and help you become responsible for your own life. Until we come to the place where we own our own problems and quit blaming them on others, we will not reach our full potential.

We have all read, or heard about, Booker T. Washington. He was born in 1856 as a slave in Virginia, and became the founder and principal of the Tuskegee Institute, a school that became famous as a model of industrial education for blacks. Washington had every reason for not becoming successful. Even when freedom came to him, he had no real tools for success: no money, education or racial privilege. In his early life, he worked in coal mines and salt furnaces, but something inside of him drove and compelled him to succeed. This something is what I like to call spirit; a realization, if you will, that we cannot let the experiences of our past control us that we must use them to learn and grow. It is an attitude which says we will control where we go and not allow the negative influences of our past to overshadow our present

One of the most difficult things in life is to take a good look at ourselves or, better yet, to allow a group of others to help us take this look. What we discover is amazing! There is truth to the theory that only by interacting with others can we really come to grips with who we are. Many people go through life without ever examining who they are, what they believe, or why they believe it. Others may examine these things occasionally. But to grow and be relevant, we must constantly examine who we are and what we believe, as well as why we believe it.

As a college professor, it was my privilege to work with young people who were bright and capable but often not in tune with who they were or why they wanted to be what they were studying to become. They thought of their future as having a particular job that would bring in enough money to allow a certain standard of living, but they had not examined the psychological or philosophical reasons that motivated them to choose that job.

My fellow psychology professors and I decided that our students needed some clinical experience early in their educational pursuits. So with the cooperation of a local hospital and chaplain, we designed a clinical experience for our students. They visited patients and wrote about how the visits affected them, then discussed themselves and their experience in group. The sessions helped them process who they were and why they dealt with life the way they did. In general, the sessions helped them to see themselves at a depth to which they had never before been exposed. For the first time, they saw themselves through the eyes of their peers and saw their peers through each other's eyes.

As you can imagine, for most of these students this was a time of growth, letting go of pain, and insightfulness. The program, however, had one serious flaw in that none of the professors had been through this kind of experience. We taught psychology, theology, and other related fields but we hadn't experienced what our students were now experiencing. So a colleague and I decided to do a summer's residency in clinical work and experience what our students had. I would like to tell you that it was easy and fun, but I must confess that it was enlightening, it was also painful.

For example, we were accustomed to being in charge of classrooms and of the courses we taught. Having studied psychology and human nature in depth, we actually, did the residency because we felt it was wrong to require students to do something that we ourselves had not experienced. We thought we were going through this in order to understand a process, but in the process, we discovered ourselves.

There were fourteen people in our group. The supervisor was a woman who had the concern of a mother but the tenacity of a pit bull! She made sure that we came to grips with our issues and helped us along the road to being fully human in a world where most people like to play pretend and ignore reality.

One of our group participants really interested me, and I want to share some of his life story and issues with you. I will call him Jim, because his story is personal. But I think you will find it is typical. Here is a short sketch of his developmental years. Jim grew up in a quaint New England town with two sisters. He was the middle child. As he was growing up, his mother had a lot of affinity for the two girls, but didn't have a great deal of understanding of the needs of a young boy. His father was a lawyer who was active in the political machinery of his state. He had achieved financial success, but felt his son needed to earn his own way so he could discover, firsthand, what life was all about. He had not been a successful athlete, but wanted young Jim to be one.

Jim worked hard to please his dad, but never was able to do so. Jim's mother took him to ballgames, but his dad was too involved with other aspects of his life to spend time with his son. Jim told our group, with great feeling, about the day he hit the home run that secured the state championship for his school and the only praise he received from his dad were the words, "Well it's about time." It's no wonder Jim felt he could never do enough to make his Dad like him.

When Jim was seventeen, his dad died from a massive heart attack. Sadly, Jim was never able to tell his dad how he felt, nor was he ever able to meet his father's expectations. Not until one day in group, did he begin to see what had been driving him all of his life and begin to heal.

Jim was a Seminary student. His most outstanding characteristic was that each time he was about to succeed at something, he would do something to ensure that he would fail. One of his favorite such tricks was to start drinking. You can imagine the response of a seminary when one of its students was caught drinking! He would also deliberately skip taking tests and would then, of course, fail.

As he was confronted by peers about his life, he realized that he was still angry with his dad because of his dad's lack of care and concern for him. Jim's desire to fail was a direct affront to his father who had been so success driven. It was only when he realized that his father, who by now had been dead for six years, was still controlling him that Jim was able to deal with his responses to life.

I wish I could tell you Jim was finally cured, but he still

struggles with the same feelings of rejection he had when he was young. There is, however, one tremendous difference. He has taken full responsibility for his actions and become a successful business man. He is comfortable with who he is and is a good father who spends time with his children. Jim could have gone through life constantly failing although he had all the potential for success. But he overcame near total inability to cope with the anger he felt towards his father. And once he believed he had potential in his own right, he began to succeed. He is an interesting example of what happens when we give others the power to control us.

Now, let me share with you a part of my own experience. I was in the sixth grade, we were required to take woodworking. My father enjoyed making furniture as a hobby. I must say, the end products were beautiful, often made from native cherry. Whenever I helped, my job was sanding, which I hated. In shop class that year, I made a simple pair of bookends out of pine boards with a birch log mounted on them. I flocked the back of the book ends with green. Thus my poor workmanship was covered up, or so I thought. But I did really sloppy work, mounting the logs with nails and bending them over on the back, which displayed my lousy work.

I took the bookends home and gave them to my father, who promptly threw them away. He couldn't imagine a teacher letting such sorry work out of the school. To me, as a twelve-year-old, the act of throwing away a gift was seen as a rejection of myself. That feeling of rejection became centered around working with wood, so I no longer wanted to build or create anything in a woodworking shop. What was really happening was I didn't want to fail because I was associating feelings of rejection with failing.

Today, I enjoy making furniture (but still don't like sanding), and I occasionally have to throw away something that doesn't turn out correctly, or start again and make it work. However, I'm okay with failing now, because I know that, in our failures we learn how to do things correctly the next time, which gives us the incentive to continue on in life.

While we are talking about failing, are you aware that many bright, capable young people fail in their school work? Teachers and parents wonder why this happens, when often, the issue of control is at the core of the problem. Many times children who are rigidly controlled by their parents will do poorly in school, because the parents can't force them to do good work. Thus, they feel that they retain control over some aspect of their life.

Well, you say, so what? We all have problems and what can I do about it anyway? The answer is: you can do something about it and you're the only one who can. Begin to ask yourself some tough questions, like, "Why do I blame others when I fail?" or "Why am I so angry about the way life treats me?" As you wrestle with questions like these, you come face to face with yourself and, if you will be honest with your answers, you will grow.

In 1965, I was drafted into the Army and I was always proud of the fact that I was drafted and didn't join voluntarily. With the Vietnam war beginning to escalate, I wasn't really thrilled with the whole idea. But the letter I received claimed that my "friends and neighbors" had selected me to represent them, so what choice did I have? I went, of course. After all the letter also said that if I didn't show up they would come and get me!

The first place I saw in my Army career was Fort Dix, New Jersey. It was also the last place I saw when I left the Army. Coming in and going out through Fort Dix left permanent impressions about Army life in my mind, but the two years between taught me many lessons of value. During my time in the service, I met many different kinds of men, from tough to tender, from ridiculous to sublime. Of them all, there was one type of individual I found difficult to understand. These were men who had been drafted, just like thousands of the rest of us, but they were angry at life and at having been drafted. Instead of making the best out of their circumstances, they fought against their situations each and every day.

When they were drafted, they assumed the rank of private, and they never progressed in military rank. They allowed the circumstances to control them, and control them they did. There were opportunities for everyone. We traveled, not always to the countries we would have chosen, but we traveled. For those who accepted responsibilities, there were promotions, a little (and I mean little) more money and greater privileges. We had not chosen to be there, but some of us made the most out of the circumstances in which we found ourselves.

Thus it is with life. We often do not find ourselves in the circumstances we would like. All of us could complain about problems we experienced as we grew up, and our children will find reasons to complain as well. But we must learn to begin from where we are today, and grow day by day.

It is also important to learn to cope with the problems life brings. Little coping mechanisms can bring big results for our overtaxed emotions. An Army buddy of mine, who had also been drafted, devised his own way of dealing with what he felt was military foolishness. He would salute with his left hand when he thought no one would notice. It was his way of saying, "I'll cooperate, but you will never totally own me."

It's time to quit blaming Mom and Dad and get on with life. First, own your problems, listen to feedback from others, and never quit believing in yourself and never quit growing. If you don't believe in yourself, other people will not believe in you, either, and will not treat you with respect. Second, find someone else who will also believe in you, someone who believes that people basically have something to offer. Third, learn to focus upon the things that are positive around you and diminish the things that are negative. As you begin to do this a strange thing will happen. You will find that the people who have been so negative in life no longer hold the same kind of influence over you, and they will begin to perceive you differently and treat you in more positive ways.

Lastly, you must keep in mind that you are not going to give others the power to determine who you are or what you become in life. Negative people will always abound but they must not be allowed to control the way in which you see yourself.

"The illiterate of the 21st century will not be those who cannot read and write, but those who cannot learn, unlearn, and relearn."

— Alvin Toffler

Make personal accountability a core value in your life. Be independent and responsible for your own well being. Take responsibility for the consequences of your choices. We all fall for the blame game, complaining, and procrastination at some time in our lives. What will you do to eliminate these dangerous traps and improve your life?

What can I do?

BEATING THE BLAME GAME

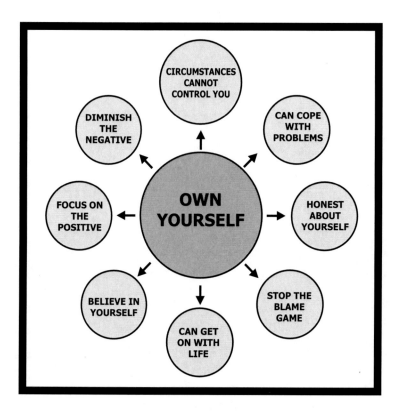

"Man cannot make circumstances for his purpose, but he always has it in his power to improve them when they occur."

Thomas Paine

CHAPTER 7

HEAR ME! HEAR ME! HEAR ME!

"Trust is the foundation of leadership."
Michael Estep

If you have ever traveled to foreign countries, then you know how frustrating it can be to get from one place to another. We spent three weeks in Europe on our way to Africa one year, and thoroughly enjoyed ourselves until we went to France. Being somewhat fluent in German had enabled us to get around most of Europe. But when we arrived in Paris and none of us spoke a word of French, we were lost. Wanting to visit certain historical places while unable to express ourselves so that we could be understood left us feeling frustrated. How often in life we feel this same frustration with those who speak the same language or even live in the same house?

Being able to express ourselves clearly and have others fully understand what we are saying is a desire we all posses, but it is something that we must work at if we are to succeed. There are a number of skills to be learned if clear communication is to take place. We will explore those paths and help you to understand how to use them, but first let's look at some preliminaries.

If you are to be believed, then what you say and what

you do must be in harmony or you will not be trusted. Let me illustrate. During the Vietnam War, the official word from our government didn't match the reality of what was taking place overseas. Our soldiers in Vietnam knew they were being lied to, and a tremendous moral problem resulted. If there is not unity in what is being said, then people will assume that none of what is being said can be believed.

Another obvious prerequisite is that body language must be in harmony with what is said. There are all kinds of formulas that tell us what part of communication is verbal and what part is nonverbal, but the reality is that the major part of any communication is what your body says.

Body language is wonderful to watch once you have learned to understand it. Through physical movement and stance, people display, their true feelings about an issue without even knowing they have done it. Having said these things, I would like to develop five levels of communication that will show how we can truly learn to communicate.

The following diagram best illustrates these levels of communication:

UNDERSTANDING AND BEING UNDERSTOOD

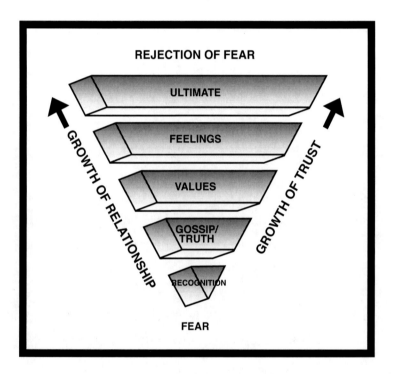

"Men often hate each other because they fear each other;
they fear each other because they don't know each other;
they don't know each other because they cannot
communicate; they cannot communicate
because they are separated."

Martin Luther King, Jr

Starting at the bottom of the pyramid, where there is no revelation of who I am as a person, is simple recognition communication. We acknowledge that people exist, but do not carry the relationship beyond that point. We often ask people, "How are you?" But if they were to begin telling us, we would wonder what their problem was.

There is a tribe in South Central Africa which greets strangers in a unique and honest way. The first person to speak will say (loosely translated), "I see that you exist," and the other person replies, "I see that you exist." No real communication takes place, just recognition.

The next level of communication I call the "gossip and truth about others" level. Here, people are willing to talk about what someone else has said or repeat some gossip they've heard about someone else. Perhaps the reason for this is that trust has not been established between the communicating individuals. In other words, I am not sure what you will do with information, then I will be very careful about what I share. So I will talk about what someone else has said or done, instead.

We all experience this level of communication every day. People who are too frightened to reach out and share themselves find it more comfortable to talk about what others have said, and done, rather than talking about themselves. There is nothing intimate about this level of communication, so it is always safe. We use this level to hide who we really are, or because we are unsure what someone might do with our personal information. It is interesting that within all of us is a certain measure of insecurity we do our best to hide from one another. Only by using others as the focus of our conversation, are we able to commune with one another.

When we move to what I call the "values" level, we begin to share more about ourselves with others. At this level, we begin to communicate our thoughts and understanding of life. It is a difficult transition, because we open ourselves up to the possibility of rejection, and no one likes to be rejected. In fact, feeling rejected makes people wish they had never become vulnerable! They revert to the second level and begin once more to talk about others. We want to feel safe, and we will do everything to stay that way.

But if we want our relationships to grow, we must trust and share our thoughts and feeling with each other. From such sharing, trust will grow. We must remember always to ask ourselves how important certain relationships are to us. It seems to me that a major problem in society today is that most of our relationships never reach deeply into the values level. Most are unsure about how to develop meaningful relationships. We've had no training in human relations, so we struggle with our own humanness.

As we move into the "feeling" level, communication becomes much more difficult. Yet, if we really want to share our feelings with others, we must be able to describe how we feel about what happens to us in our relationships. Most males, in our society are at a definite disadvantage, because we were constantly reminded as children that men don't show emotions. And most of us were told over and over that men don't cry. So we learned to stifle our emotions and let our intellects rule us.

A man I know was in a group therapy session when someone said something negative about him. The group leader asked him how he felt about the remark. He replies, "I'll have to think about it." In other words, he had shut down his emotions and was unwilling/unable to get in touch with them.

If you feel yourself becoming too critical of this man, then try to describe some of your own feelings. For example, describe what "love" feels like to you. Some people would say the word gives them warm, fuzzy sensation. Others would say the word makes them feel "butterflies" in their stomach. But most people are at a loss for words that truly describe their feelings. They will use words like "caring," "concern," and "support," but those are "brain" words that don't describe feelings. And if we can't describe our feelings, then we can't communicate them.

Most people feel they can describe anger, because it has been acceptable for them to display some level of anger during most of their lives. The reality is, however, they still are not truly able to describe their angry emotions. Instead of saying something like, "When I get angry, I feel like I am on fire and my stomach is churning," they use other words such as "furious," or "mad" which only say the same thing.

In fact, most people cannot identify what they are feeling, because they have shut off their emotions for so long that they are no longer in touch with their feeling. Let me give you an extreme example.

A young family I know had everything going for them. The husband was successful in his chosen profession and the wife had put her career on hold in order to raise their two young children, a boy and girl three years apart. When the children were five and three years old, doctors discovered that their mother had cancer. Over the next five years she grew worse, and ultimately passed away, leaving her husband with a ten-year-old and seven-year-old to raise.

The day his wife was buried, he sent his children back to school with the comment that they needed to get on with life. Don't get the wrong message; he loved his wife dearly, but he did not know how to respond to what he was feeling, let alone how to identify those feelings. Five years later, I met this man because our professions brought us together. He had remarried and seemed to be in control of his life, but the control was only a mask. The anger, hurt, and disbelief he felt over life having been so cruel as to take away his first wife was still foremost in his mind.

One day, as we were talking, he began to share his life experiences and nearly skipped over the loss of his first wife. I brought him back to the incident of her death and began to express sympathy for his loss. It was as if a mighty volcano erupted, as tears flowed and sobs shook his body. Finally, he expressed his long repressed, emotions and began to heal.

He told me that he was afraid of his emotions, because while he was growing up, he was never allowed to show them. He was told over and over that he must learn to control his feelings. He thought he had done so, but for years, they had controlled him until he felt like a caged lion. He still struggles, and he will always be one of the walking wounded. But he is much happier today, and so are his children and second wife. A part of himself that he had tried to ignore almost destroyed him. But because he moved beyond thinking into feeling he was finally able to communicate on both levels.

When I share with you my feelings, I have opened a door to my being for you to walk through. Opening the door takes away my masks and lets you know the real me. Please don't criticize or laugh at what I feel, because that's who I really am, and your rejection will only make me less willing to trust. True, I only open the door to my intimate feelings for those who share their feelings with me, but acceptance feels so good to give and to receive, that I don't want to go through life without it.

The last level of communication is one I like to call the "ultimate" level. This is one in which we can be totally open and honest with who we are. At this level, we are free to talk about our failures, as well as our successes. To be totally ourselves without fear of rejection is the ultimate product of this level. It seems to me that this is where two people who are married ought to be functioning.

A word here about families would seem to be in order, because most family relationships break down as a result of poor communication. Family members, fear of rejection keeps them from expressing themselves, which ultimately leads to the rejection they fear. It seems, then, that some simple tools are necessary to help us communicate well with each other. So here they are:

1. Send clear messages that include your feelings as well as your thoughts, and put them in words another person can understand.

2. Choose a place to communicate where there are few or no distractions, so you can concentrate on and hear the full message.

3. Make sure the other person understood your message, by asking for feedback from him or her.

4. When the other person responds to what you said, use good listening skills and don't frame a reply before he or she finished.

Practicing these four basic skills will enhance your relationships and help you grow as a person.

As this chapter on communication closes, I want to deal with the issue of trust. In order to trust, we have to take risks. When we disclose our feelings and thoughts to someone else, we run the risk of rejection so some people will never open up.

Many children want so badly to be accepted that they lie to their parents and say only things they think will be pleasing. The end result is they lose their identity and never know who they are.

The process of trust must be based on a mutual willingness to reveal and risk. In order to do this, we must have a certain level of confidence in the other person in the relationship. In the beginning, there is a minimal level of disclosure. Then, as both parties reciprocate thoughts, feelings, and openness, the level of trust deepens.

The opposite of this process is true, as well. When one person feels rejected, ridiculed or disrespected, or when one refuses to disclose his or her thoughts and feelings, then high levels of trust cannot exist.

Communication, communication, communication. That's what good relationships are made of. Communication helps us to grow as humans and see ourselves through the eyes of others. It also enables us to become fully human.

We are constantly learning and exposing ourselves to new information and ideas that can change our ways of thinking.

Create healthier relationships, prosperity and abundance, spiritual growth and a meaningful life purpose through communication.

Regularly ask yourself, "Why am I ...?" Listen closely for the answer that surfaces in your mind, then write it down.

CHAPTER 8

EYEBALL TO EYEBALL

*"You can give without loving, but you
cannot love without giving."*

Mark Graham

Conflict management. The very concept of dealing with conflict fills many people with anxiety. Somewhere along the way, they picked up information which led them to believe that good relationships don't have conflict, which they believe to be negative and unnecessary. Often, however, they find themselves in the midst of conflict and they assume that there must be something wrong with them. The truth is, however, that conflict is a normal part of life. Wherever two or more people are together, there is the potential for conflict. People come from a variety of family backgrounds, religious beliefs, educational levels, etc. If conflict can be viewed as merely the presence of tension in relationships and honest differences in perspective, then we will be well on our way to seeing it as a useful tool in human relations.

Many have had the experience of being friends with someone, perhaps very close friends, only to have the relationship end over unresolved conflict. A friend once told me an incident from his life which illustrates this vividly. He and his friend had grown up and gone to school together.

During their eighth grade year, something happened to change their friendship for years. I say "something" because neither one of them could remember the event that brought about the separation. All they remember is at some point they began to dislike each other. The event that caused the problem was forgotten, but the two boys began to dislike each other. In fact, they often found themselves disagreeing on issues and events to the point of having physical altercations.

Years later, they met again, this time in the military, where they had to depend on each other. They gradually discovered that they really liked each other and became fast friends once more. My point is that unresolved conflicts create problems broader and more far reaching than they should have, meaning that conflicts need to be resolved when they arise.

Self is often the greatest deterrent to successful conflict management. By that, I mean one's level of self-esteem contributes to his or her ability to resolve conflict. The higher people's self-esteem, the more willing they will be to consider a number of solutions to the conflict. On the other hand, the lower their self-esteem, the more likely that people will not settle for any solution but their own. For them, a rejection of their idea is taken as a rejection of themselves, so they fight to have things their way. When you consider that upwards of ninety percent of people suffer from low self-esteem, you begin to get a picture of our dilemma.

Over the years, I have served on a number of committees and found it very interesting to watch people at work, especially how they are often unable to see a big picture and will fight only for what they want. Every issue becomes an opportunity for them to prove to themselves that they are valuable. Company needs or group goals become insignificant. Win/lose becomes the issue, and they feel that they must win in order to preserve self.

It seems to me that we must come to the place in our society where we recognize that people are more important than things. You may say, that's a given. But I would have to disagree. We live in the age when we are told to worry only about number one, not to let anyone step on us, and we must do whatever it takes to be top dog. Only when people, and the building up of people becomes a priority in our lives will our success be certain.

If the world has learned anything from the life of Mother Theresa, it is that treating everyone with dignity, regardless of his or her station in life, brings world-class acclaim. Why? Because it's what we all truly need, but have a hard time doing for others. But we get caught up in the lesser issues of life and forget what is most important. "Reconciliation" describes the conflict resolution process. It allows us to work through conflict in caring and loving ways and, at the same time, resolve the issues. It allows relationships to remain intact and develops a greater sense of interpersonal caring among people.

Let me take you through the conflict resolution process and explain it as we go. The first question you must resolve is, "How important is the relationship to me?" Not every conflict is worth resolving. In fact, we often become embroiled in petty spats because they seem safe and we can vent feelings that actually belong to a different issue than the one at hand.

For example arguing with a rude store clerk seems senseless to me. That relationship is of no importance. If you are at the checkout counter in a grocery store and the cashier treats you rudely, just leave the goods on the counter and walk out. In today's world, there will be six more stores on your way home that want to sell you the exact same goods and will appreciate your business. So don't allow every minor disagreement to become an opportunity for conflict. Remember: the more important the relationship, the more essential it is that I resolve the conflict.

Once you have established that a relationship is important to you, it's time to do some soul searching. Ask yourself the question, " In what manner do I usually deal with conflict that can hinder the conflict being resolved?" There are basically five ways that people handle conflict. Let's explore them and see what method you use most often.

The Runner: believes that it is impossible to resolve conflicts, and feels conflicts should be avoided at all costs. Runners believe that the only result of a conflict will be damage to a relationship. As a result, their relationships lack depth. They have learned to escape both physically and psychologically, and will avoid people that they are in conflict with.

The Fighter: wants to overpower an opponent. Fighters see every conflict as a win-lose struggle and they always want to win. These individuals are motivated by their own goals, and they will use other people to make sure they succeed. If by some chance, their opponent seems to be winning, they will attack and try to overwhelm him or her.

The Martyr is always willing to give in and accept responsibility for any conflict. Relationships are so important to martyrs that they will put aside all personal goals in order to keep a relationship intact. They will do all they can to avoid conflicts or even pretend that one doesn't exist, in order to maintain peace and harmony. No matter what else happens, they want to make sure to preserve their relationships.

The Compromiser is concerned about both relationships and goals. They want to find the middle ground in any problem and try to work things out. It is important to them that both sides be seen as winners, so the solution they seek is between the two extremes. With compromisers, goals and relationships take a back seat to resolving the issue.

The Confronter values his or her own goals and relationships, as well as the goals and relationships of others. Confronters view conflicts as issues to be resolved in a way that achieves the highest good for both parties in the conflict. They view conflict as an opportunity to buildup people and their self-images through affirmation and resolution. Confronters feel that open and honest confrontation is the only way to achieve conflict resolution when relationships and goals are equally important.

Consider the following diagram:

CONFLICT MANAGEMENT

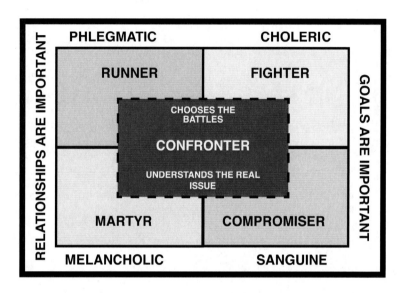

"You can get everything you want if you help enough others get what they want."

Zig Ziglar

As we look at the ways in which people handle conflict, it is easy to see that we need to learn to confront conflicts where the relationship and goals are important to us. However, because temperament styles and family backgrounds and issues vary so widely, that most individuals do not know how to approach confrontations.

The next step in resolving conflict is to define it, so we can clearly understand what it is about. In doing this, we have to use guidelines. We must learn to describe other people's actions and make sure the conflict is over issues and actions rather than personalities. Next, we must identify our mutual actions that create and maintain the conflict. Always keep in mind that we don't want to get into a win-lose struggle, that our goal is to mutually resolve the conflict.

Once we understand what the conflict is about, we can confront the other person. Keeping in mind that confrontation is not the same as showing hostility. It is the task of sharing what one person perceives the conflict to be about while at the same time giving positive affirmation to the individual with whom he or she is in conflict. This is not an opportunity simply to vent and not allow the other individual to respond. It is the time when good open communication takes place. For my part, I try to communicate all my thoughts and feelings openly about the conflict, and then allow the other person to do the same. Then comes the hardest part of all: I don't demand that the other person change. The problem with solving conflicts is that most of us want our own way, and automatically assume that the version of the conflict that we see is correct so the other person must change. Only when we sit down together and develop a joint definition of the conflict, will we begin to see both sides of the issue. Once both of us have input into the definitions we can begin working on resolution.

In resolving a conflict, there are a number of things to keep in mind. First, you must remember to deal with issues rather than personalities. It is impossible for a person to defend attacks against personality. For example, if the other party says the problem is that you are stupid or flighty or whatever, then there is no way to resolve the problem.

Once the issues are laid out, we can discuss how each party in the conflict will behave differently in the future. I find it helpful at this point to actually sit down and write out the issues and the agreement. Doing this allows us to modify the agreement should it become necessary. But, more importantly, defining, resolving, and writing down the details allows us to develop our conflict management skills much more quickly.

In resolving our issues, we must also take into account what the cost will be if the conflict is unresolved, and how we will respond if one of us who is involved messes up.

I know these steps seem like a lot of work. That's true. But as you become more proficient at resolving your issues, you will be amazed at how your relationships will deepen and your sense of self-esteem will be heightened. Empowering yourself and others to live at the highest level of being is the greatest thing you can do for and with your life.

Before we leave the topic of conflict management, I want

to show the relationship between an individual's temperament and his or her usual way of dealing with conflict.

Choleric: This individual is by nature a fighter who always wants to win. Cholerics have a difficult time negotiating anything, because their goals are of primary importance.

Sanguine: This is the other goal-oriented temperament. Sanguines want to achieve, but it is also important that people like them. In fact, they are willing to compromise in order to achieve their goals, but they will also use people to make themselves look good.

Melancholy: This is the temperament with the martyr complex. Melancholies want people really to like them, and they strive to help others reach their goals while denying their own. They tend to be perfectionist, but are very sensitive to other people and their needs.

Phlegmatic: This individual is a runner. The Phlegmatics level of drive appears to others as if he or she is unwilling to make decisions. The truth is, however, they are very loyal to relationships and will do anything to keep them intact.

These are the reasons why we should all learn to practice and develop the skills necessary to handle conflict management well. There are also obvious reasons that many people don't want to get involved. But to ignore the chance to resolve conflict is to deny ourselves and others the possibility of and opportunities for growth.

"...look at that word "blame." It's just a coincidence that the last two letters spell the word me. But that coincidence is worth

thinking about. Other people or unfortunate circumstances may have caused you to feel pain, but only you control whether you allow that pain to go on. If you want those feelings to go away, you have to say: 'It's up to me.'"

— Arthur Freeman

What can I do?

Reveal hidden subconscious thoughts about how other people hold you back.

Clarify who you are and what you want. Feel confident and passionate about who you are as you clearly identify what personal conflicts matters most to you.

Check on your motivations regularly.

CHAPTER 9

PAVLOV'S DOG

"God gives us the ingredients for our daily bread, but he expects us to do the baking."

William Arthur Ward

Many believe that behavior modification is the only method that will ensure long-term change in people's attitudes and actions. As with Pavlov's dog if something is repeated and practiced often enough it will become the norm for the person involved. Behavior modification is truly a powerful tool, but it's only one of three that I am going to focus on.

In case you don't know the story, the late Russian physiologist Ivan Pavlov trained a dog to salivate every time a bell rang. Pavlov did this by feeding the dog when the bell rang. Of course, human beings are not dogs, but we can be "trained" to react to certain stimuli. However, I believe there is more to be gained by using a composite approach to personal well being.

That is why I want to tell you about the three elements that make up the Triad of development and reorientation. Those change elements are Behavioral, Affective, and Cognitive. Used together, they can create an opportunity for a new and different outlook and approach to life. I call this the "Sphere of Balance." Assuming that a picture is worth a thousand words, let me illustrate it this way:

THE SPHERE OF BALANCE

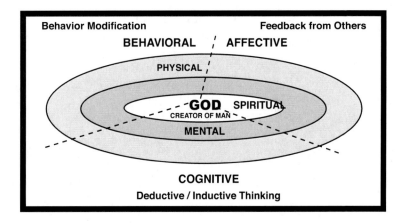

"His momentous achievements are rarely the result of a clean forward thrust but, rather of a soul intensity generated in front of an apparently insurmountable obstacle which bars his way to a cherished goal."

Eric Hoffer

Because behavior is learned, it can be changed or unlearned. Where you grew up; who your parents were; how many siblings you had, are only a few of the elements that made you who you are today. Certain types of behavior were allowed or not, depending on what was acceptable to the adults responsible for you. Oversight from friends, relatives, and communities helped to round out your understanding of right and wrong.

Your brain stores this behavioral information and, as you repeatedly act in certain ways, the behavior becomes your norm. Over time, we create neural pathways in our brain that makes our behavioral response almost automatic. The good news is that neural pathways can be changed. This means that you can learn to behave differently.

Behaviorism as a theory of psychology came into being in the late 1930s and early 1940s. Its core beliefs are that humans are trapped in a society and mentally are controlled by it. What you see, what you hear, and what you repeat is what you become. However, like Pavlov's dog, through the use of reward or punishment, you can be changed.

Unfortunately, this theory, this methodology, this practice of psychology is what has led us to the idea that people are not responsible for their actions, including crimes they may commit. In other words, society has trained them to act in certain ways, so society is at fault. Our K through 12 educational system is burdened with behavioral problems because this pervasive psychological theory is carried to the extreme.

A critical element is ignored in this theory, however. This element, which changes not only outcomes, but also the research itself, is the belief that there is a God who creates and then cares for his creation. It contends that man is not just a highly evolved biological being, but both a physical and spiritual being. Faith in a creator, a being more powerful than humans, one who desires our best, gives us hope, which is essential to change.

It is not my purpose or desire to discuss or define God, but the widely held concepts of God that are prevalent in society today make beliefs difficult. (My next book will deal with the question of who God is and how to understand the relationship He desires to have with humanity.)

With behavior modification as our goal and understanding that we are products of our environment, we can learn new behaviors by practicing them. First, you must see that your behavior is harming you in some way, perhaps in your relationships. Then, you must desire to change and begin working on those changes immediately. Experts say lasting changes take place during 28 days of constant practice. Let me illustrate with this simple example. Most of us have a certain route we drive as part of our daily routine. There are other routes we could take, but this one has become the most comfortable for us. What would happen if, for the next month, we were to take an entirely different route and be faithful in taking the new route every single day. At the end of a month of traveling the new route will seem as comfortable and familiar as the old one .

We can change self-destructive behaviors in the very same way. Stop-smoking clinics and the twelve step program for AA work on this principle, by allowing participants to practice new ways of seeing themselves and acting out new behaviors that can change their lives. Believing that you are not an accident of time, but a child whom God deeply loves makes this journey less lonely and much more meaningful. So I advise you to choose an attitude, behavior or action you want to change, and get to work.

The next leg in this sphere of balance is what is called Affective, or how we come across to others. Unless we listen to the feedback that others give us, it's difficult to understand the effect our approach has on them. I am not saying you must change who you are, but I am saying that you must understand yourself. The goal is to utilize your greatest strengths and minimize your weaknesses.

The way we treat people and the way they perceive our treatment of them is often not the same. Having friends that will be honest with you and give you feedback will be very helpful. However, don't be offended by what they say; rather listen and try hard to hear what they are saying to you about yourself.

The third element that makes up the sphere of balance is cognitive functioning. What I am talking about is the learning process and the ability to use your brain as your greatest asset. Learning to think through problems in rational ways by using inductive and deductive thinking will help you make good decisions. This comes back to the issue of education.

Do not cheat yourself in life by dropping out of school and not finishing your education, because your potential to accomplish your goals is directly related to your education. If you didn't study hard when you were in school; get help and learn what you need to know now. Your goals are just that, yours. So get going, and don't let anything keep you from achieving, your goals!

Remember that your perception of yourself is your reality. Your perception can change the moment you begin practicing these three elements of the Sphere of Balance:

BEHAVIORAL

AFFECTIVE

COGNITIVE

ABOUT THE AUTHOR

Dr. Greenlaw is the founding and current President of Florida Hospital College of Health Sciences. Dr. Greenlaw holds baccalaureate, masters, and doctoral degrees in religion. He has been a professor of religion at two colleges. For six years he and his family lived in Zimbabwe where he taught religion and ministerial education at Solusi College.

In addition to leading Florida Hospital College from its inception, Dr. Greenlaw helped found the American Consortium of Schools of Health Science. He is known for his vision, his entrepreneurial spirit, and his sense of humor. Understandably proud of the growth of the College, Dr. Greenlaw is a family man who is most proud of his wife, two daughters, and three grandchildren.